LET IT GO

How to stop Suffering over what you can't Control and Finally be at Peace with Yourself

Dedication

To everyone who's ever felt tired of trying to fix what was never theirs to fix.
To those who held on too tightly.
To those who carried too much.
To those who forgot themselves while trying to hold the world together.

This book is a reminder:
You deserve lightness.

Copyright © 2025 by Adrian Cantero

All rights reserved.

No part of this book may be reproduced, stored in a retrieval system, or transmitted in any form or by any means — electronic, mechanical, photocopying, recording, or otherwise — without prior written permission from the author.

This is a non-fiction work. The experiences and reflections shared are personal and do not replace professional advice or guidance.

Published by Adrian Cantero – Independent Author

Distributed by Amazon KDP

First Edition – 2025

Table of Contents

Introduction

Chapter 1 – The Day I Got Tired of Pleasing Everyone

Chapter 2 – You Don't Have to Convince Anyone

Chapter 3 – The Weight That's Not Yours (But You Still Carry)

Chapter 4 – When You Let Go, Life Starts to Flow

Chapter 5 – Emotional Freedom Is a Daily Choice

Chapter 6 – What Others Think Isn't Your Problem

Chapter 7 – Let Them Talk. Let Them Go. Let It Be.

Chapter 8 – You Weren't Born to Be Accepted — You Were Born to Live

Chapter 9 – How to Stop Trying to Control Everything

Chapter 10 – The Lightness of Living for Yourself

Chapter 11 – How to Love Without Losing Yourself

Chapter 12 – Let It Go. Go Live.

Final Note from the Author

Introduction

There comes a moment when you're just… tired.
It doesn't matter how much you try, how hard you chase, how desperately you work to be accepted, loved, understood.
It never seems to be enough.
Something always feels out of place — and someone's always expecting you to be someone you're not.

It was in that exact moment that a simple idea hit me like lightning:
Let it go.

Three syllables. Two words. One release.

This book was born from that phrase.
And no — it's not just another pretty quote for Instagram.
It's a key. A turning point. A shift in direction.

From here on, you'll start to see life differently.
You'll learn that you don't have to control everything.
You don't have to save everyone.
You don't have to be perfect all the time.

More than that:
You'll relearn how to live for *you*.
You'll take the weight off your shoulders.
You'll make room for lightness to enter.

This isn't about being selfish.
It's about becoming whole again.

Shall we begin?

Chapter 1

The Day I Got Tired of Pleasing Everyone

I remember exactly where I was.
The room was silent, but my mind was a storm.
The kind of silence that screams on the inside.
I was smiling, nodding, fitting in… but it didn't feel like me.

For a long time, I believed that pleasing others was the way to be loved.
I said yes when I wanted to say no.
I listened when I wanted to speak.
I accepted when I was ready to give up.
All to keep the peace — even if it cost me a war inside myself.

The truth is, I was afraid.
Afraid of disappointing people.
Afraid of being rejected.
Afraid of being alone.
And that fear made me wear masks every single day —
Masks of confidence, of friendliness, of control.

Until one day, I just… got tired.

It wasn't some big event.
It was a moment. A crack.
A wave of exhaustion so deep I couldn't pretend anymore.

I looked in the mirror and barely recognized myself.
Who was that person who always put everyone else first... and forgot his own name?

That day, I didn't scream. I didn't cry.
I just decided: never again.

Never again would I ignore how I felt.
Never again would I shrink to fit.
Never again would I carry the burden of pleasing everyone and lose myself in the process.

That was the first step to my freedom.
It was the moment I realized that choosing yourself is choosing to truly live.
And that's when my journey back to myself began.

At first, it felt weird.
Because when you stop pleasing others, the world doesn't know what to do with you.
Some people pull away.
Others criticize.
You start hearing things like:
"You've changed."
"Wow, now it's all about you."
"You've become selfish."

But I learned something powerful:
Being called selfish by those who benefited from your lack of boundaries isn't offensive.
It's freedom.

The people who get most upset with your growth are often the ones who thrived off your self-abandonment.

That's when you realize:
Pleasing doesn't equal love.
Saying yes to everyone, all the time, isn't kindness — it's self-erasure wearing a smile.

So I started practicing saying no.
And at first, it hurt.
Saying no to someone you love — especially when they're used to hearing yes — can feel cruel.
But then you realize: saying no to others is often the biggest yes you can give to yourself.

"No, I can't right now."
"No, that doesn't feel right to me."
"No, I don't want to go down that road."

And each honest no gave me back a piece of myself —
A piece I had traded for crumbs of acceptance.

Through that process, I began to uncover who I was without the masks.
And I saw clearly who truly loved me — not for what I did for them, but for who I really was.

Life started to feel lighter.
More real.
More mine.

Little by little, I started connecting with people who vibed on the same frequency —
People who wanted me around not out of convenience, but out of truth.
People who didn't get offended by my boundaries, but respected them — even admired them.

If there's one thing I've learned, it's this:
You don't need to be everything for everyone.
You just need to be whole for yourself.

And believe me, when you choose yourself, the universe starts to show you how everything changes.

So if today you're feeling tired of pleasing, know this:
That tiredness is a sign.
A signal that you're waking up.
It's the beginning of something new — a return to home... to yourself.

You weren't born to be an extension of everyone else's desires.
You were born to be you —
With all that you feel, all that you believe, and all that you choose.

The world doesn't need more perfect people.
It needs more real ones.

And being real starts with one simple, powerful act:
Telling yourself — enough.

That's what I told myself that day.
And I never looked back.

If you're going to please someone, let it be your soul.
If you're going to give in, let it be to your heart.
If you're going to follow a path, let it be your own.

Since then, I've been relearning. Tripping. Adjusting.
But with one deep certainty:
Trying to please the world is a slow death.
Living for yourself…
That's when life truly begins.

Reflection – Chapter 1: The Day I Got Tired of Pleasing Everyone

What became clear here?

The need to please others is rooted in fear —
Fear of rejection, of not being loved, of letting people down.
But constantly trying to be who others want you to be leads to one thing: self-abandonment.
When you start choosing yourself — even if it bothers those who were used to your "yes" —
you finally begin to truly live.

Key phrase:

"Saying no to others is often the biggest yes you can give to yourself."

What you can take with you:

The people who truly love you will respect your boundaries.

Being real is more important than being perfect.

You can't please everyone — and trying to will only drain you.

The first step to finding yourself again is simply saying: Enough.

Practical exercise:

Reflect for a moment:
How many times in the past few days have you said "yes" when you really wanted to say "no"?

*Write down at least 3 situations like that —
and think about what you could do differently next time.*

Chapter 2

You Don't Have to Convince Anyone

How many times have you wasted your energy trying to make someone understand you?
How many times have you overexplained, justified your feelings, begged to be seen, heard, embraced?

We often carry this belief that we need to convince others we're good enough —
That we have worth. That we deserve love.
But the more you try to explain yourself, the more drained you become.

You don't need to convince anyone of what you feel.
Those who want to understand you will listen with their heart.
Those who don't — wouldn't hear you even if you drew them a map.

Here's the truth: not everyone will understand you.
And that's okay.
Not everyone will value you.
And that's okay too.
Not everyone will stay.
And yes — that's okay as well.

Your mission in life isn't to prove anything to anyone.
Your mission is to live at peace with your own truth.

Of course, it hurts when someone doesn't get you — especially when that someone matters to you.
The longing to be accepted, embraced, validated… it's human.
But if you build your life around that longing, you'll be stuck in a constant battle with yourself.

How many times have you softened your tone, changed the way you dress, or held your words — just to avoid seeming "wrong"?
How many paths have you walked away from, simply because you were afraid of what others might think?
How many times have you silenced your truth to keep a relationship, a friendship, a job?

And in the end, what's left?
An emptiness.
A growing distance from yourself.
A hollowness — even when surrounded by people.

Trying to convince others is like chasing the wind.
Because those who are meant to truly see you won't need explanations — they'll only need your presence.

And this is the heart of it all:
You need to be whole on the inside, even if the outside world keeps trying to reshape you.
That inner wholeness is what protects your peace when

everything around you is just noise.
And there's no argument more powerful than your authenticity.

True peace begins when you accept that you won't please everyone.
That being misunderstood is part of the path.
That being judged is unavoidable.
But being true to yourself? That's freedom.

You don't need to justify every choice you make.
You don't need a PowerPoint presentation for your emotions.
You don't need to turn your life into a defense speech.
Your existence is valid — just as it is.

Sometimes, what saves you... is silence.
It's knowing that the time you spend trying to convince someone could be used to care for yourself, to grow, to create, to love yourself better.

And here's the irony:
The moment you stop trying to convince others, you start attracting the exact people who see you clearly —
No effort. No filter. No performance.
It's in that space of truth where real relationships are born.

Some people listen only to reply.
Some only look so they can judge.
Some are present just to demand.
But then there are those rare ones — who see you.
Who understand you in silence.
Who don't need a translation.

Before seeking to be understood, seek to understand yourself.
Before seeking acceptance, accept yourself.
Before looking for validation, validate your own worth.

You are whole.
And those who see that — they'll walk with you.
Those who don't — will fall away.
And that's okay.

So today, before you try to convince anyone of anything, stop and ask yourself:
Do I believe in me?

Because when you believe, you don't need to prove.
When you trust, you don't need to shout.
When you accept yourself, the rest starts to matter a lot less.

Don't waste your energy trying to win the heart of someone who never made room for you.
Use that energy to boldly take up space in the life that was always meant to be yours.

You don't need to be understood to be real.
You don't need applause to be whole.
All you need is to look at yourself with love and say:
I am enough. I hear myself. I respect myself.

And believe me — the silence of those who don't get you is nothing compared to the peace of living in truth.

At the end of the day, what really matters isn't who understood you —
It's who stayed.
Even without understanding everything…
They stayed because they respected who you are.

That's priceless. That's freedom.

Reflection – Chapter 2: You Don't Have to Convince Anyone

What became clear here?

Living your life trying to convince others of your worth is like chasing the wind —
It drains you, it hurts you, and it pulls you away from yourself.
But when you validate, accept, and respect yourself,
you realize you don't need an audience —
you just need peace.

True freedom begins the moment you understand that you don't owe anyone an explanation for being who you are.

Key phrase:

"Those who see you with their heart don't need arguments.
Those who don't want to see you wouldn't understand — even with subtitles."

What you can take with you:

People who truly love you don't demand constant explanations.

Your worth doesn't depend on being understood.

Living authentically matters more than being accepted by everyone.

Sometimes, silence is the greatest act of self-love.

Practical exercise:

Think of a recent moment when you over explained yourself.
Now reflect:
Did you do it out of fear of being misunderstood —
or because you didn't fully trust your own voice?

Write one self-affirming sentence you could've said in that moment.
Example:
"My truth doesn't need defense. It stands on its own."

Chapter 3

The Weight That Isn't Yours (But You Still Carry)

There are wounds that didn't begin with you — but you carry them as if they were your own.
There are weights life placed on your shoulders without ever asking if you could handle them.

Family expectations.
Friends' frustrations.
Inherited guilt.
Borrowed fears.
Silent shame no one ever spoke about — but you felt it in your skin.

From early on, we're taught to carry it all:
What's ours, what's not, what no one else wanted to hold.
And without even noticing, your soul gets filled with baggage you never chose.

But eventually, your body gets tired.
Your mind screams.
Your chest tightens.

And in that moment, you have to stop and ask yourself:
"Is this really mine?"

Because what isn't yours weighs differently.
It presses harder.
It weakens you.
And worst of all:
It keeps you from living light.

There's guilt that isn't yours — but you inherited it.
There's silence that isn't yours — but you learned to accept it.
There's pain that was born long before you — but they taught you it was your job to heal it.

Maybe you grew up being told you had to take care of everyone.
That you had to handle it.
That you had to be strong — always.
So you became an adult thinking that being "good" meant carrying the world on your back,
even when you could barely hold yourself up.

But there's a difference between empathy and overload.
Between compassion and self-abandonment.
You can love someone deeply — and still not carry their weight for them.

Carrying what's not yours feels like walking around with an invisible backpack.
At first, you think you can handle it.
Then you start to slow down.
You lose your breath.
You lose direction.

Until one day, you realize…
you don't even know who you are without that weight.

And that's where the process of liberation begins.

Letting go doesn't mean ignoring other people's pain.
It means recognizing that you feel too.
That you matter too.
That you also need space to breathe.

You have the right to set down what was never yours to carry —
and to keep only what strengthens you.

That's not selfish.
That's self-care.
That's emotional sanity.

You don't have to save everyone.
You don't have to fix every problem.
You don't have to be the safe harbor for those who never offered you shelter.

Some weights, when you finally release them, don't bring guilt —
they bring relief.
And that relief is your soul telling you:
You're finally coming home.

Lightness begins with this act of courage:
Letting go of what doesn't belong to you.

Not to escape —
but to finally live with free hands and a whole heart.

      Maybe you need to relearn how to live without the weight.
To believe it's possible to walk without guilt.
To believe it's okay to say, "I can't carry this,"
and still be worthy of love and respect.

      You're not weak for letting go.
You're strong for realizing… you don't need to anymore.

      And if someone gets upset about that —
they were likely benefiting from your exhaustion.

      You weren't born to be the foundation for everyone else.
You were born to be whole.
And sometimes, being whole means letting go.
It means saying no.
It means choosing yourself.

      So set it down.
Take a deep breath.
And begin again — lighter.

      Because life doesn't have to be carried.
It's meant to be lived.

Reflection – Chapter 3: The Weight That Isn't Yours (But You Still Carry)

What became clear here?

So often, the exhaustion we feel doesn't come from what's truly ours —
but from what we're carrying for others.
Inherited guilt, imposed responsibilities, pain that was never ours to begin with.
Letting go isn't selfish — it's an act of self-respect.
You don't have to carry it all.
Only what makes you stronger.

Key phrase:

"Some weights, when you let them go, don't bring guilt — they bring relief."

What you can take with you:

You have the right to let go of what was never yours to carry.

Love isn't about overloading yourself for someone else — it's also about knowing when to protect your peace.

Strength doesn't mean carrying everything — it means recognizing when something hurts you.

Letting go of certain burdens might be the beginning of your next chapter.

Practical exercise:

Grab a piece of paper and write:
"What am I carrying that doesn't belong to me?"

List 3 situations, guilt trips, or pressures that came from others —
and that you feel ready to release.

Then, read it out loud and say to yourself:
"I give myself permission to set this down. I choose to walk light."

Chapter 4

When You Let Go, Life Starts to Flow

Some things only begin to happen once you stop trying so hard.

As long as you're forcing it, life gets stuck.
As long as you're holding on to what's already over, there's no room for the new to arrive.
As long as you're trying to control every detail, lightness gets shut out.

But when you let go...
everything changes.

The answers come.
Connections realign.
What's true stays.
What was heavy begins to dissolve.

Letting go isn't giving up.
It's trusting.
It's saying: "I did what I could. Now I let life do its part."

It's in that space of surrender that good things happen —
The right people show up.
The doors open.

Love blooms effortlessly.
And peace… finally breathes.

      Have you ever noticed how a river flows better when there are no rocks in the way?
Life works the same way.
Letting go is removing those rocks.
It's letting it all flow.

      But letting go takes courage.
It means accepting that you can't control everything.
That some things aren't about effort — they're about timing.
That not every door you're trying to force is closed forever.
Some just aren't yours.

      We were taught to fight, to insist, to chase.
And yes — persistence is noble.
But sometimes, pushing too hard becomes a prison.
And knowing when to stop — that's wisdom too.

      There are relationships you're trying to save alone.
Paths you're trying to force by yourself.
And it's draining you.
It's drying you up inside.

      Because real connection only exists when it's mutual.
When it flows both ways.

      Letting go opens space for the truth to show up.
For life to reveal what's real, what serves you, what lifts you.
And also — what needs to be left behind.

Letting go is also about releasing control over the future.
About not needing to plan every single detail.
It's about trusting that what's meant to be, will be.
In its own time.
In its own way.
With the ease and grace you deserve.

It's understanding that everything has a cycle —
And that honoring the endings is also a way to welcome new beginnings.

Maybe today you're holding on to something.
A relationship. A job. An idea. An expectation.
Holding on because you're afraid of the void.
Afraid of what comes next.
Afraid you won't find anything better.

But the void isn't always emptiness.
Sometimes, it's the space something new needs to be born.
Something you can't even imagine yet —
Something that may be exactly what you've been waiting for…
but it couldn't reach you while your hands were still full of the old.

Letting go isn't a lack of love.
It's self-love.
It's respecting your limits.
It's choosing to stop hurting for something that no longer holds you.

Breathe.

Trust.

Let go.

Life knows the way.
And when you release control, it will take you exactly where you're meant to be.

Let life surprise you.
Let the unexpected find you.
Let what is light lead the way.

You deserve to live with a free heart.
With a calm soul.
With the kind of peace that only arrives when you stop forcing — and start flowing.

Reflection – Chapter 4: When You Let Go, Life Starts to Flow

What became clear here?

So often, life doesn't get stuck from lack of effort — but from too much insistence.
Letting go isn't giving up —
It's trusting the flow.
It's making space for the new, the light, the true to arrive.

Lightness begins when you understand that trying to control everything isn't freedom — it's a cage.

Key phrase:

"Letting go isn't a lack of love. It's self-love."

What you can take with you:

Not everything needs to be forced. What's meant for you flows naturally.

Persistence is noble, but knowing when to let go is wisdom.

The emptiness you fear might be the very space where something new is ready to grow.

Trusting life is an act of faith in yourself.

Practical exercise:

Close your eyes and ask yourself honestly:
"What am I still holding on to that I already know I need to release?"

Write down one situation, relationship, or expectation that's been draining your energy.

Then, write this sentence:
"I release this with love. I trust what life has in store for me."

Breathe. Trust. Let go.

Chapter 5

Emotional Freedom Is a Daily Choice

Some days, everything feels light.
You wake up calm, take a deep breath, and feel in control — of yourself, of life, of the moment.

And then there are days when chaos takes over.
Anxiety tightens.
Fear knocks.

What's the difference between these two days?
It's not what happens on the outside.
It's what you choose on the inside.

Emotional freedom isn't a destination — it's a practice.
A choice.
A commitment you make to yourself, every single day.

It's like brushing your soul's teeth:
Every day you clean out the thoughts that don't serve you,
release the guilt that doesn't build you,
and let go of the weight that isn't yours.

You may not control what you feel,
but you can choose what you do with what you feel.

That's emotional maturity.
That's strength.

Being emotionally free means feeling everything —
without being ruled by any of it.

It's holding space for sadness without drowning in it.
It's laughing wholeheartedly, without needing laughter to survive.
It's loving deeply, without erasing yourself.
It's getting frustrated, without falling apart.

It's a practice.
And like any practice, it takes repetition.

It's looking inward with honesty and asking:
"What am I feeling today? Is this really mine? Or something I picked up from the world around me?"
Because often, the heaviness you feel isn't even yours —
It's a collection of voices, pressures, and expectations that slipped in without you noticing.

Emotional freedom doesn't mean living without pain.
It means learning how to move through pain with awareness.
It's having inner tools that keep you from drowning in your own emotions.

It's knowing that your thoughts aren't facts.
That your anxiety isn't a sentence.
That your anger doesn't define who you are.

It's giving a name to what you feel —
without letting it dictate your actions.

There will be days when the world feels gray.
When nothing fits.
When everything weighs heavy.
And on those days, more than ever, emotional freedom means choosing gently.

Choosing not to be so hard on yourself.
Choosing to speak to yourself with kindness.
Choosing to slow down — even when life speeds up.

It's in those moments that we need to hold ourselves the most.
To be our own shelter when the world feels like a storm.

Maybe no one notices how hard you try just to stay standing.
Maybe no one understands the silent battles you fight every day.
But you know.
And that alone is reason enough to hug yourself tighter.

Emotional freedom is a practice of self-knowledge.
The more you know yourself, the more you understand your limits.
The more you recognize your triggers.
The more you learn to protect yourself — without shutting down.

And that doesn't make you cold.
It makes you conscious.

It's you — at the center of your life.
Not as someone who suppresses,
but as someone who chooses with intention.

So when the day feels heavy,
when your mind is loud,
when your heart starts to doubt...

Pause.
Close your eyes.
And remember:

You have a choice.
You have power.
You have the right to live light — even when the world tries to pull you under.

Choose you.
Every single day.
Even when it's hard.
Even when no one gets it.
Even when it feels small.

Because that daily choice —
is what changes everything.

And if today happens to be one of those hard days,
breathe.
Treat yourself with compassion.

Take care of yourself with patience.
And remember:

    You've made it this far.
And that alone says so much about your strength.

Reflection – Chapter 5: Emotional Freedom Is a Daily Choice

What became clear here?

Emotional freedom isn't a destination —
it's a daily practice of choosing yourself, over and over again.
Being free doesn't mean you stop feeling —
it means you're no longer ruled by what you feel.
And even when the world gets heavy,
you can still breathe, pause, and respond with awareness.

Key phrase:

*"You may not control what you feel,
but you can choose what you do with what you feel."*

What you can take with you:

Embracing your emotions is an act of strength, not weakness.

Thoughts are not facts.

Emotions don't have to become automatic reactions.

Self-awareness and self-compassion go hand in hand.

Choosing yourself — even on the hard days — is emotional freedom.

Practical exercise:

Today, pause for a moment and ask yourself honestly: *"What am I feeling right now?"*

Write it down with no filter — like a private journal entry or a raw confession.
Then ask yourself:
"Is this feeling truly mine — or did I absorb it from the outside?"

Take a deep breath.
And write down one kind and gentle choice you can make for yourself today.

Chapter 6

What Others Think Isn't Your Problem

You can do everything right.
Be kind. Be real. Be generous.
And still — someone will criticize you.
They'll judge your steps, question your intentions,
and create a story that doesn't belong to you.

And you know what?
There's nothing wrong with you.

Other people's opinions are just that: opinions.
They are not absolute truths.
They don't define who you are.
And they should never run your life.

Once you understand that — everything changes.

You stop trying to please everyone.
You stop wasting energy trying to be understood all the time.
You stop giving so much weight to what comes from the outside
and start listening to what rises from within.

Because no one else lives your life.
No one else feels what you feel.

Carries what you carry.
Dreams what you dream.

So why let someone outside dictate your choices?

If you live for other people's approval,
you'll lose yourself.
You'll suffocate.
You'll dim your own light.

But when you let go of that, a new kind of peace is born —
A peace that comes from being true to yourself.
From knowing you don't need to prove anything.
That you don't owe anyone anything.
That you weren't made to fit into anyone's mold.

What others think? That's their business.
You've got something more important to take care of:
Your own truth.

Yes, it hurts to be misunderstood.
It hurts when someone makes something up about you.
It hurts when they reduce your story to a mean comment.
But you can't live your life trying to correct every false perception.

Some people — even with the truth staring them in the face —
will still choose to believe the lie they created.

This world is full of judgment.
And often, the ones who judge the loudest
are the ones most afraid to look within.
Because it's easier to point fingers
than to face your own reflection.

And you?
You don't need to carry their projection.

Knowing that is freedom.
Because it allows you to walk lighter.
To live more authentically.
To choose your next step based on your own conscience —
not the approval of someone who doesn't know your path.

What others think is about them —
The filters they use to see the world.
The beliefs they carry.
The pain they project.

You are not responsible for any of that.

You are responsible for being honest with your own feelings.
With what you believe.
With how you live.
That's what real freedom is.

And don't get it twisted —
Living authentically doesn't mean living without criticism.

It means knowing exactly who you are —
even when the world tries to label you as something you're not.

Peace comes when you understand that your truth
is worth more than any story someone else creates about you.

So when you hear judgment — breathe.
Remember who you are.
Remember what you've lived through.
Remember what you feel.
And keep going.

Your story is far greater
than the opinion of someone who only saw a piece of it.

Don't waste your energy trying to fix someone else's thoughts.
Use that energy to build a life with more presence,
more integrity,
and more self-love.

Because in the end,
the only opinion that truly needs to matter — is your own.

Reflection – Chapter 6: What Others Think Isn't Your Problem

What became clear here?

You can be real, kind, and full of integrity —
and still be judged.
But what others think of you says more about them than it does about you.

True freedom begins when you stop living to be understood
and start living in peace with your own conscience.

Key phrase:

"Your story is far greater than the opinion of someone who only saw a piece of it."

What you can take with you:

- Other people's opinions do not define your worth.
- Trying to please everyone is the perfect way to lose yourself.
- Judgments reflect more about the other person than they do about you.

- Peace comes from living in alignment — between what you feel and what you choose.

Practical exercise:

Think of one judgment that hurt you or held you back.

Now write:
"That opinion belongs to them. I don't need to carry it."

Then, write three truths about yourself — things no one can take away, no matter how much the world tries to twist your story:

- I'm honest about what I feel.
- I stay true to what I believe.
- I am free to be who I am.

Chapter 7

Let Them Talk. Let Them Go. Let It Be.

Have you ever noticed how much time and energy we spend
trying to control things that were never ours to control?

What someone says.
Whether they stay or leave.
Whether they understand or criticize.
Whether they support you — or turn their back.

But there's one thing that changes everything:
Letting.

Let them talk.
Let them think.
Let them go.
Let it be.

You don't need to hold on to what doesn't want to stay.
You don't need to keep insisting on someone who doesn't value you.
You don't need to carry someone who doesn't want to walk beside you.

Life flows better when you understand that control is an illusion,
and your role is simply to move forward —
even if some people don't come with you.

Let them talk.
Those who speak about you without knowing you
are speaking more from their own pain than from your truth.
Those who judge your journey without knowing your story
are only revealing their own insecurities.

Let them go.
Some people were important —
but they were never meant to stay forever.
And that's okay.
Gratitude for what was.
Maturity to move on.
It's not about abandonment —
It's about evolution.

And finally, let it be.
Let the world move as it will.
Let life bring what's meant for you,
take what isn't,
heal what hurt,
and reveal what still needs to be seen.

Letting is liberation.
Letting is trust.
Letting is making space for the new to arrive.

You'll only live light
once you stop holding on to what should have been released long ago.

The truth is:
Some people were only in your life to teach you something.
Others, to show you what you no longer deserve.
And some — simply to lead you to a new level of awareness…
and then leave.

Letting go isn't a lack of love.
It's self-love.
It's recognizing that holding on to what hurts you
isn't care — it's self-cruelty.

Sometimes, the peace you're searching for
is hiding behind that one thing you're still holding onto.
A habit. A pattern. A cycle.
A hope.
A version of the past.

Letting go might hurt —
but holding on to what's already over hurts much more.

Yes, people will talk.
They'll judge.
They'll laugh.
They'll doubt you.
But life doesn't pause for those who don't understand your process.
And neither should you.

You don't owe explanations for moving forward.
You don't owe apologies for choosing your peace.
You owe only one thing:
honesty with yourself.

Let them talk.
The voice of those who judge
will never echo louder than your own truth.

Let them go.
You are no one's prisoner.
Your life doesn't need to be anchored to anyone who isn't lifting you.

Let it be.
Because when you let go, life starts to align.

Sometimes the very thing blocking your next step
is what you're still refusing to leave behind.

You deserve to walk light.
You deserve relationships that add, not drain.
You deserve spaces that nourish you — not suffocate you.

Letting go is also about choosing who continues the journey with you.
It's understanding that not everyone fits into your next chapter.
And that's okay.

Life isn't about clinging —
It's about flowing.

So, if today someone hurt you —
with words, with absence, with indifference…
let it go.

Not out of weakness.
But out of strength.
Because now you know that your energy is worth more than reactions.
Worth more than convincing.
Worth more than proving something to someone who never wanted to understand.

Let it go.
And take care of you.

Take care of your peace.
Of your silence.
Of this new version of you that's emerging.

You only need one thing to keep going:
The courage to let go.

And it already lives inside you.

Take a deep breath.
And let it be.

Reflection – Chapter 7: Let Them Talk. Let Them Go. Let It Be.

What became clear here?

Life asks for lightness.
But lightness only comes when you let go.
Letting go isn't weakness — it's maturity.
It's self-protection.
It's self-love.

Not everyone will understand you.
Not everyone will walk beside you.
And that's okay.
Letting go creates space —
For peace.
For the new.
For what truly adds to your life.

Key phrase:

"You'll only live light once you stop holding on to what should have been released long ago."

What you can take with you:

You don't need to keep insisting on people who've already left.

Letting go is also love — love for yourself.

Those who speak about you without knowing you are revealing more about themselves than about you.

True strength is letting go without needing permission or explanation.

Practical exercise:

Grab a piece of paper and write:
"What — or who — am I still holding on to out of fear of letting go?"

Then, write a short letter (you won't send it), saying:
"Thank you for what it was. But now, I let you go. I choose my peace."

Read it out loud.
Then, if you feel ready, tear it up or burn it — to symbolize this closure.

Let go.
And feel the lightness arrive.

Chapter 8

You Weren't Born to Be Accepted — You Were Born to Live

Acceptance is a trap dressed up as praise.

Sure, being recognized feels good.
We feel seen, valued, loved.
But the problem begins when the need for acceptance becomes a condition for your existence.

That's when you start shaping your words, your actions, your dreams...
just to fit into someone else's expectations.
And without realizing it, you stop living — and start performing.

But let me remind you:
You weren't born to entertain an audience.
You were born to be whole —
even if it makes people uncomfortable.
Even if they don't get it.
Even if they criticize you.

You didn't come here to be accepted.
You came here to live.
To live for real.

With depth.
With courage.
With truth.

    Life is not a showcase — it's a plunge.
And those standing on the shore judging
will never understand the bravery of those who dive in.

    Stop shrinking yourself to avoid rejection.
Those who reject you for being yourself
are simply making space for those who will love you honestly.

    Being accepted is nice.
But being free — that's much better.

    And freedom only comes when you realize that living for yourself
matters far more than applause from people who don't even know the real you.

    The trap of acceptance is subtle.
It starts with compliments, with encouragement,
with that natural desire to be liked.
But little by little, it shapes your steps, your choices, your voice —
until one day you look in the mirror
and barely recognize who you've become.

    It's like you're performing on a stage —
saying rehearsed lines,
wearing clothes others picked out,

suppressing your feelings just to keep the peace.
But deep inside... you're fading.
Because nothing suffocates more than living just to please.

Have you ever said "yes" when you wanted to say "no"?
Laughed at something you didn't find funny?
Agreed to something — a plan, a favor, a situation — just so you wouldn't upset someone?

Those are the small signs
that you're living more for others than for yourself.

Living to be accepted is living only halfway.
It's trading the truth of your soul for the comfort of fitting in.
And eventually, the cost becomes too high.

Rejection hurts — yes.
But self-denial hurts even more.
It's quieter.
Slower.
Deeper.

You don't need to be understood by everyone.
You don't need to be liked by everyone.
You don't need everyone's approval.

What you do need...
is to be true to yourself.

And there's a deep beauty in that.
Because when you're faithful to who you are,
you start to attract what's real too.

Your relationships change.
Your conversations deepen.
Even your gaze shifts.

You begin to be surrounded by people who truly see you —
who accept you with no filters,
who don't demand a polished, edited version of who you are.

That is freedom.

Life is too short to waste energy trying to fit in.
Too precious to be shaped by other people's opinions.
Too valuable to be spent trying to belong in places that were never yours.

You are not a product on a shelf.
You are life — raw and pulsing.
You are a process.
You are depth.
You are beautiful in your imperfection.

So if today you feel like you're losing yourself just to be accepted —
breathe.
Come back home to yourself.

Remember who you were before the world told you who you "should" be.

And if someone walks away when you show them your truth —
be grateful.
Because real love doesn't ask you to wear a mask.

You weren't born to be shaped by others.
You were born to shape,
to create,
to express,
to live with soul.

Choose your authenticity.
Choose your truth.
Choose your peace.

You are enough —
whole,
real,
human.

There's no freedom greater than living with a heart free
from the need for approval.

And if you are to be accepted,
let it be by those who truly see you.
But above all —
let it be by yourself.

Reflection – Chapter 8: You Weren't Born to Be Accepted — You Were Born to Live

What became clear here?

Constantly chasing acceptance means giving up your own truth.
When you live to please, you slowly lose pieces of yourself —
until you no longer know who you are.

But living authentically — even if it makes others uncomfortable,
even if it scares you —
is the only real path to a life that feels true.

You weren't made to fit in.
You were made to be whole.

Key phrase:

*"Being accepted is nice.
But being free is so much better."*

What you can take with you:

- The need to please is a prison — with invisible walls.
- Rejection hurts. But self-rejection hurts even more.

- Authenticity drives away what's not real — and that's a blessing.
- You don't need to be approved.
You need to be you.

Practical exercise:

Write down 5 situations where you felt like you were *"hiding"* or acting just to be accepted.

Then, for each one, write a recovery statement like: *"Next time, I'll choose my truth."*

Close your eyes and repeat out loud:
*"I'm not a role to be played.
I'm a life to be lived."*

Chapter 9

How to Stop Trying to Control Everything

Trying to control everything is the most exhausting illusion there is.

We try to predict, organize, and anticipate every step.
We plan every conversation, every move, every possible mistake —
all in an attempt to avoid pain, rejection, failure.

But living with the need to control everything
is like trying to hold water in your hands.
The tighter you squeeze, the more it slips through.

The problem is that we confuse control with safety.
We believe that if we have everything under control,
nothing will go wrong.
But life is not an exact equation.
It's movement. It's unpredictability. It's surprise.

And that's okay.
It's okay not to know what's going to happen tomorrow.
It's okay to not be sure.
It's okay to trust.

Letting go of control doesn't mean abandoning responsibility —

it means stopping the self-torture of trying to predict what isn't yours to control.

Of course, you can plan, dream, organize.
But do it without rigidity.
Without attachment.
With space for the unexpected.
With openness to what wasn't in the script.

Some of the best things in my life happened off plan —
They came when I stopped fighting
and started flowing.

Letting go of control means trusting life — and trusting yourself.
It means knowing that whatever happens,
you'll handle it.
Because you already have —
you've handled things you once thought you couldn't.

But this urge to control often comes from a deep fear:
The fear of suffering.
The fear of getting hurt.
The fear of repeating old wounds.

We try to control people, outcomes, situations
because the unknown terrifies us.
But we forget:
It's in the unknown that life actually happens.

Some people even try to control love —
Measuring words.
Calculating feelings.
Planning reactions.
But love doesn't fit into a formula.
Not in life, and not in us.
Love overflows.
It messes things up.
And that's where the beauty lives.

You don't need a perfect script.
What you need is presence.
Surrender.
Faith in the journey.

Letting go of control means making room to trust:
That whatever comes, you'll know how to handle.
That whatever leaves, was never really yours.
And that what arrives — will arrive whole.

It's like dancing with life,
instead of against it.

Yes, make your plans —
but don't cling to them.
Plan with an open heart.
With flexibility.
With the wisdom of someone who knows
that the best things in life are often not what you imagined —
but what life reveals.

Because many times, when control falls,
creativity blooms.
Love flows.
Truth shows up.

You weren't born to manage the universe.
You were born to feel.
To explore.
To learn.

When you let go, you allow yourself to be surprised.
And some of the greatest blessings of your life
will come from exactly what you didn't plan.

Letting go is hard because we've been trained to protect ourselves.
But real protection comes from trust —
Trust in yourself.
Trust in timing.
Trust in what life brings.

You will make mistakes.
You'll stumble.
You'll change your mind.
And that's okay.
That's not chaos — that's growth.

So today, if anxiety tightens,
if fear tries to trap you,
if that need to control everything comes rushing back…
breathe.

Remember:
You've faced the unexpected before.
You've made it through things you thought you couldn't.
You've survived days that felt impossible.

You are living proof
that letting go isn't about losing.
It's about setting yourself free.

So breathe.
Let go.
And keep going.

Life takes care of those
who walk with courage —
not with control.

Reflection – Chapter 9: How to Stop Trying to Control Everything

What became clear here?

Trying to control everything is a trap that drains your soul.
The more you try to predict and dominate,
the further you drift from presence, from faith, from real life.

Letting go of control isn't giving up —
it's a gesture of trust.
It's understanding that the unexpected can carry blessings too.

Key phrase:

*"Living with the need to control is like trying to hold water in your hands —
the tighter you squeeze, the more it slips through."*

What you can take with you:

- Control is an illusion born from fear.
- The unexpected is where life truly blooms.
- You don't need to know what's coming next —
  only trust that you'll know what to do when it comes.

- Planning is healthy.
  Clinging to the plan is not.

Practical exercise:

Write down:
"What am I trying to control out of fear of losing it?"

Now answer:
"What would happen if I simply chose to trust?"

Close your eyes and repeat:
"I release control and welcome whatever life has for me."

Chapter 10

The Lightness of Living for Yourself

Living for yourself isn't selfish —
it's being honest with your own existence.

How many times have you put someone else's life ahead of your own?
Postponed a dream, swallowed a truth, silenced a desire —
all to avoid disappointment, to keep the peace,
to be what others expected?

But there comes a point when your body gets tired,
your soul starts to scream,
and your heart grows heavy.
And then you realize:
if you keep living this way,
you'll reach the end of your life with the painful feeling
that you never really lived at all.

Living for yourself is about reclaiming your story.
It's remembering who you were
before trying so hard to please everyone else.

It's reconnecting with what moves you,
what stirs your heart,
what makes you feel alive.

It's choosing the clothes you actually like.
The routines that make sense to you.
The silence that soothes you.
The people who lift you.
The dreams that pull you forward.

Living for yourself means putting yourself first —
without guilt.

It means understanding that you're the only person
who will be with you until the very end.
And if you don't take care of yourself,
no one else can do it for you.

You can't outsource your happiness.
Or your peace.
Or your identity.

Lightness begins when you allow yourself to simply
exist as you are —
without needing to prove, explain, or ask for permission.

And no, it's not easy at first.
Because society pressures.
Family pressures.
Culture teaches us that thinking of ourselves is selfish.
That we must give, sacrifice, adapt.
But living like that slowly makes you sick.
You start to disappear —
until all that's left is a shadow of who you used to be.

When you finally decide to live for yourself,
people around you might get confused.
Some will say you've changed.
That you're cold.
That you've grown distant.

But those who truly love you —
they'll understand.
They'll support you.
They'll stay.

You weren't born to fit into molds that suffocate you.
You were born to create space.
To open paths.
To dance to the rhythm of your soul.

Lightness isn't the absence of problems —
it's the presence of truth.
It's knowing that even in chaos,
you are respecting yourself.
You are being loyal to who you are.

It's saying "no" without guilt.
Asking for help without shame.
Stopping without feeling useless.
Choosing silence when the world gets too loud.

The lightness of living for yourself is found in the details —
In sleeping well because you were honest.
In laughing at something simple.

In sipping coffee without rush.
In walking down a street and feeling the wind
like it's the first time.

Lightness lives in dropping the act.
In looking in the mirror and finally saying:
That's me.
Whole.
Flawed.
Real.

You don't need to prove anything to anyone.
You don't need to rush.
You don't need to compete to feel worthy.

You just need to remember that living is an act of courage —
and living for yourself is the greatest act of all.

So if today you're wondering where to begin...
begin with you.
With the outfit you want to wear.
The "yes" you want to give.
The "no" you need to say.
The break your body is asking for.

You deserve a life that makes sense to you —
even if no one else understands it.
Even if it seems crazy.
Even if it's different from what they expected.

Your heart knows the way.
And when you listen,
lightness arrives.

Not like magic —
but as a natural consequence.

Because those who live for themselves
don't live lighter because everything is perfect —
they live lighter because everything is true.

And that changes everything.

Reflection – Chapter 10: The Lightness of Living for Yourself

What became clear here?

Living for yourself means stepping out of the autopilot of others' expectations
and stepping into the rhythm of your own truth.
It's not rebellion. It's not escape.
It's emotional maturity.

Lightness doesn't come from the absence of problems —
it comes from being aligned
with what you feel and how you live.

Key phrase:

"Living lighter isn't about having fewer problems — it's about living with more truth."

What you can take with you:

Life is too short to abandon yourself.

No one else is going to live your life for you.

Those who truly love you will respect your choice to live for yourself.

Lightness lives in the small daily acts of staying true to yourself.

Practical exercise:

Grab a pen and paper and write:
"Which areas of my life are still shaped by what others expect of me?"

Then ask yourself:
"What is one thing I can do today — no matter how small — just for me?"

And then, do it.
Give yourself that gift.

Chapter 11

Loving Without Losing Yourself

Loving someone is one of the most beautiful experiences in life.
But when love requires you to dim your light,
it stops being love — and becomes a cage.

It's not love if you have to shrink to fit.
If you have to stay silent to avoid conflict.
If you have to hide who you are just to keep someone close.

Real love doesn't suffocate.
It doesn't demand that you sacrifice your essence.
It doesn't treat your freedom as a threat.

You can love someone deeply — and still stay whole.
You can care for someone — without forgetting yourself.
You can make compromises — without abandoning who you are.

The problem starts when we confuse giving with erasing ourselves.
When we think love means constantly reshaping ourselves.
When we're so afraid of losing someone,
we lose ourselves first.

But let me remind you:
The right love will never ask you to disappear.
It will walk beside you.
It will uplift you.
It will respect your space and embrace you as you are.

You deserve to love — and to be loved —
with ease. With reciprocity. With truth.

And if staying close to someone requires stepping away from yourself,
that person is not a companion — they're a prison.

Loving without losing yourself is one of the highest forms of emotional maturity.
And maybe… the greatest gift you can give to yourself.

Because love begins in you.
It grows in you.
And it only overflows when you're full — of yourself.

How many times have you reshaped who you are out of fear of being alone?
Accepted less than you deserve?
Swallowed your feelings to avoid conflict?
Disappeared quietly, hoping someone would finally love you?

True love doesn't need you to vanish.
It wants you to shine.
To grow.

To feel safe being your full self — without fear of being abandoned for it.

Healthy relationships aren't built on control — but on space.
Space to be.
To feel.
To evolve.
Space to disagree.
To change your mind.
To be vulnerable.

If you have to ask for permission to exist in a relationship, something is wrong.
If you have to hide just to be accepted,
they don't love you — they love the version of you they made up.

Love is not a cage. It's shared freedom.

You can build a life together
without giving up your own life.
You can make plans as a couple
without abandoning your individual dreams.
You can listen to the other
without muting your intuition.

The greatest proof of love is staying whole next to someone —
and allowing them to stay whole, too.
No suffocating.

No controlling.
No reshaping.

    Love is building, not owning.
Partnership, not dependence.
Presence, not pressure.

    When you love yourself enough,
you won't accept anything less than respect.
When you know yourself,
you won't force yourself where you don't belong.
When you value yourself,
you'll know: love that demands your absence
isn't worth your presence.

    Loving without losing yourself means being able to say "no" without fear.
Setting boundaries clearly.
Asking for space when you need to breathe.
Keeping your individuality alive — even inside a union.

    If a relationship monitors your every step,
questions your every choice,
pulls you away from your friends,
disconnects you from your truth —
that's not love.
That's control disguised as care.

    And you deserve more.

You deserve a love that lifts you — not locks you down.
That listens — not silences.
That accepts — not corrects.

So if today you feel small inside a relationship, ask yourself:
How much of me am I losing to keep this going?

And if the answer is "too much,"
maybe it's time to choose yourself.
To remember who you are.
To come back home.

You weren't born to live a love story
where the other person is always the main character.
You were born to be the author of your own journey —
And if someone is to walk beside you,
let them be someone who respects every page.

Love is beautiful.
But if it costs you your peace,
it's too expensive.

So breathe.
Look at yourself with more kindness.
And make this promise:
I will never lose myself again just to keep someone else.

Because true love begins
when you find yourself —

and choose yourself.
Every single day.

Reflection – Chapter 11: Loving Without Losing Yourself

What became clear here?

Loving someone should never cost you your essence. Love that requires you to disappear is not love — it's a cage. Real love is built on freedom, respect, and space for both to grow
— without fear of being fully themselves.

Key phrase:

"If you have to dim your light to keep someone close, that's not love — it's a prison."

What you can take with you:

Love is about growing together, not disappearing together.

Someone who truly loves you wants to see you shine, not shrink.

Preserving your individuality in a relationship is emotional maturity.

Saying *"no"* doesn't make you less lovable — it makes you whole.

Practical exercise:

Ask yourself honestly:
"In the love I'm living — or the love I want — how much of myself am I keeping intact?"

If the answer is "not much," write this:
"I commit to never losing myself for anyone."

Say it out loud.
And if it resonates deeply, write it on paper and place it somewhere
you can see every day — as a quiet promise to your soul.

Chapter 12

Let It Go. And Go Live.

You've made it this far.
You've read every chapter.
You allowed yourself to reflect, to feel — maybe even to cry.
And now, more than ever,
you're ready.

Ready to let go.
And ready to live.

Letting go doesn't mean forgetting.
It doesn't mean ignoring.
It doesn't mean pretending it didn't hurt.
It means recognizing, honoring, learning —
and then releasing.

Releasing what no longer serves you.
What weighs you down.
What holds you back from flying.

Life is now.
Not when everything is fixed.
Not when everyone approves.
Not when you're 100% sure.
It's now — even with fear.

Even with doubt.
Even with a racing heart, but just enough courage to take that first step.

    The life you want doesn't begin when everything's perfect.
It begins the moment you choose yourself.

    Letting go is an act of self-love.
It's finally putting yourself first — not out of selfishness,
but out of respect.

    For so long, you've held on.
You've endured.
You've swallowed tears.
Ignored signs.

    But now… it's time to take a deep breath and say:
I deserve more.

    And when you let go, the world doesn't fall apart.
On the contrary —
it realigns.
Things settle.
The pain quiets.
The path begins to open.

    Because in truth, what weighs us down most
isn't the past —
it's the attachment to what should have been released long ago.

You no longer have to be the one carrying yesterday on your back.
You don't have to hold onto what keeps hurting you.
You don't have to stay in places where you've outgrown your space.

Letting go also means accepting that not everything will make sense right away.
That some answers only show up after we find the courage to turn the page.
That the unknown is scary — but also healing.

You weren't born to stay stuck in old chapters.
You came here to evolve.
To learn.
To feel the lightness of being whole again.

Maybe what you need to release is a friendship that became a burden.
A love that became a cage.
An environment that only drains you.
A version of yourself that no longer fits.
And that's okay.

You don't have to carry eternal guilt.
You just need to respect yourself.

Life will go on — with or without the things you're clinging to.
The only difference is how you'll walk:

Dragging chains...
or spreading wings.

There's something powerful in closing cycles.
In accepting that some things have reached their time.
In letting life move forward
without needing to control every step.

Letting go is a way of honoring your journey.
Of recognizing that even though it hurt,
it taught you something.

But now, what's left — is the present.
And it's asking for space.

You don't have to rush forward.
You can go at your own pace.
But go.

Because staying where there's no life
is a slow kind of dying.

So go live.
For you.
For all that you still can be.
For the dreams you tucked away.
For the parts of yourself you forgot.
For the life still beating in your chest.

Go live the love that's waiting for you.
The discoveries you haven't imagined.
The connections that only show up when you make room.

And if someone says you gave up too easily,
that you should've tried harder,
that you were weak —
smile inside.

Because only you know the weight you carried.
And only you know the freedom of finally letting go.

The world doesn't need you in pieces.
It needs you whole.
Present.
Real.

So let it go.
The pain.
The guilt.
The expectations.
The plan that didn't work out.
The person who didn't stay.
The version of you that no longer fits.

And go live.
With less control and more surrender.
With less fear and more trust.
With less rush and more presence.

Life doesn't wait for you to be ready.
It invites you — every single day.
And you don't need to have it all figured out to say "yes."
You just need to take the first step.

  You may not have all the answers.
You may still feel the ache.
But now... you have awareness.
You have choice.
And that changes everything.

  Letting go is courage.
Living is courage.

  And today,
you have both.

  So go —
Because you deserve to live your life —
with truth, with lightness, with love.

  Go.

  Because freedom lives exactly at the point
where you finally decide to let go.

  And when you let go...
that's when you truly begin to live.

Reflection – Chapter 12: Let It Go. And Go Live.

What became clear here?

Letting go isn't weakness —
it's courage.

Letting go is an act of self-love.
It's the moment when you stop merely surviving
and finally start to live.

When you release what no longer serves you,
you create space for everything that does.

Key phrase:

*"You don't need to have it all figured out to live —
you just need the courage to take the first step."*

What you can take with you:

Letting go is an ending — but also a beginning.

What hurts today might be exactly what frees you tomorrow.

The new can only arrive when you're brave enough to let the old go.

You deserve to live whole — not in pieces.

Practical exercise:

Write down (or simply say in your heart):
*"Today I let go of what holds me back
and choose to live with truth."*

Then, take a deep breath.
Feel the lightness arrive.
And say to yourself:

"I deserve the lightness of being who I truly am."

Author's Final Note

    Writing this book was more than just a project —
it was a deep dive.
A reunion with myself.
A journey within, where every word carried pieces of my truth,
my pain, my healing.

    And none of this would've been possible alone.

    From the bottom of my heart,
I thank my wife, **Adrielle**.
You were my safe harbor in stormy days,
my quiet inspiration in long nights,
and my strength when giving up felt easier.
Every gesture of support, every word of encouragement,
every hug in the middle of chaos —
all of it lives in the pages of this book.

    To my mother, **Senaide**,
whose words, prayers, and wisdom taught me early on
the value of being true.
The roots you planted in me are now blooming in this work —
a living proof of unconditional love.

    To my mother-in-law, **Ana**,
who welcomed me as a son

and stood by me in moments when even I doubted myself.
Your presence meant more than words could ever say.

To my children, **Santiago and Victoria** —
you are the light on my path.
On hard days, all it took was a smile,
an innocent question,
or a burst of laughter in the silence
to remind me of what truly matters.
You are my biggest reason to keep growing,
learning, and letting go of what no longer fits.

I'm also deeply grateful for the falls,
the disappointments,
the closed doors —
because they taught me how to rise differently:
stronger, more aware.
And of course, for the victories,
which arrived like healing
and quiet rewards on this faith-filled journey.

This book is made of every moment I wanted to quit
—
and chose to keep going.
It's built on every "yes" I gave myself
after so many "no's."
It's made of real life,
with all its intensity, beauty, messiness, and transformation.

If you made it this far, know this:
this book now belongs to you too.

May it have spoken to your soul,
touched your heart,
and maybe — just maybe —
lit a new spark within you.

Because at the end of the day,
all we really need is…

**the courage to let go,
and the true desire to finally live.**

With all my care and truth,
Adrian Cantero

About the Author

Adrian Cantero is an entrepreneur, mentor, and father. Driven by faith and purpose, he writes from the soul to help others live with more peace, courage, and meaning.

Passionate about human transformation,
he has devoted his life to inspiring people
to let go of what hurts
and embrace what sets them free.

His words have already impacted thousands of people seeking lightness, direction, and new beginnings.

"Let It Go" is his first book —
and a heartfelt invitation to return to yourself.

Made in the USA
Columbia, SC
09 July 2025